BECAUSE OF YOU

Old Glory Flies

Poems of Gratitude for Our U.S. Military and Veterans

Written by Julie Dueker

Illustrated by Ray "Bubba" Sorensen II

Author's Note

What began as elementary history lessons, has turned into a ministry inspiring this book. As a teacher and mom, I hope to instill in my children, like my parents did in me, a spirit of patriotism and gratitude for those whose sacrifices have secured our American freedoms. My students and I love presenting programs honoring our veterans and military. We share patriotic songs and poems, and recite historical documents such as Lincoln's Gettysburg Address and the Declaration of Independence. These programs have mutually blessed us and our heroes. As a result, we've received multiple requests to perform in local community events, leading me to create Young Patriots Club (YPC). YPC is a local Christian ministry of freedom-loving youth, whose mission is to honor God and uplift American heroes.

The poems in this book were inspired by personal stories shared with us by military members and veterans, who left quite an impression on us. They were written out of gratitude and awe for all who've sacrificed on our behalf. It's my prayer that these poems will be shared by children in tribute to American heroes, by children on the laps of relatives who've served our country, and gifted by anyone with a friend or relative who has put country above self. As pages are turned, I pray God's love is felt and our heroes are honored. It's because of them Old Glory flies!

Dedicated to:

the brave men and women of the United States military
past, present, and future, to whom we owe our freedom

and

God, from whom all blessings flow

Table of Contents

Not Too Young

Too young to join the army,
Too young to go to war,
But not too young to understand
We're what you've fought for.

For us you left your families
To see that we'd be free,
For us you obeyed orders
To preserve our liberty.

Know, please know we're grateful;
To you we are in debt.
We want nothing but to honor you,
So glad our paths have met!

For you we sing our hearts out,
And thank our God above.
We may not even know your names,
Still we give you all our love!

Because of You Old Glory Flies

You say you're not a hero,
"Others have sacrificed more."
But in my heart, that's what you are –
Courageous to the core.

"The last full measure of devotion"
You are willing to give,
So whether you serve in combat or not,
A hero's life you live.

You're larger than the big screen;
Fictitious heroes battle there.
You're real and brave – you're mortal,
In human skin you dare...

To take on battles you may not win,
Obey orders, follow your call.
Scenes don't go as scripted;
Undaunted you stand tall.

So let me call you hero,
'Cause you are one in my eyes.
The simple truth – because of you,
Freedom's mine – Old Glory flies!

Bags Are Packed

Bags are packed, drills complete,
Departure's now at hand.
It's time for us to see you off,
To secure the freedoms of our land.

It's not easy to see you go;
Like you, we will be brave.
Your calling is a high one,
The stuff of which heroes are made.

We pray you off, we place you in
The mighty hands of God.
He's walked each step so far with you,
Will go every step you trod.

Watch over them, dear Father,
Keep them safe, we pray.
Wrap your love around them,
Until comes the day...

Their operation is complete,
On American soil they stand,
And we wrap our arms around them,
With love from a grateful land.

Think of Me (God)

When you're lying in the trenches, think of Me.
I'm there – be not afraid,
I will give you aid.
When you're lying in the trenches, think of Me.

Psalm 121: 1–2 ...where does my help come from?
My help comes from the Lord…

When your strength is failing you, think of Me.
I'm strong though you are weak,
When My power you seek.
When your strength is failing you, think of Me.

II Corinthians 12:9 My grace is sufficient for you,
for my power is made perfect in weakness.

Continued…

When the battle's numbed you, think of Me.
I know pain, I know it well;
To Me your troubles tell.
When the battle's numbed you, think of Me.

John 11:35 Jesus wept.

When you're far, far from home, think of Me.
Each one that you adore,
They're in My care, I love them more.
When you're far, far from home, think of Me.

*Eph. 3:18 ...how wide and long and high and deep
is the love of Christ.*

Continued…

When you're opening your letters, think of Me.
I wrote one for you Myself
Filled with all My love.
When you're opening your letters, think of Me.

Jeremiah 31:3 I have loved you with an everlasting love.

When you're returning home, think of Me.
Normal's changed, but I'm the same;
Keep trusting in My name.
When you're returning home, think of Me.

*Hebrews 13:8 Jesus Christ is the same yesterday
and today and forever.*

When you don't know what's next, just ask Me.
Trust in Me, I'll be your guide;
I'm always by your side.
When you don't know what's next, just ask Me.

*Proverbs 3:5–6 Trust in the Lord with all your heart...in all your
ways acknowledge him, and he will make your path straight.*

Continued…

When nightmares are relived, think of Me.
Blood sweat from My brow,
I know fear; I'm with you now.
When nightmares are relived, think of Me.

Luke 22:44 Being in anguish, he prayed more earnestly and his sweat was like drops of blood falling to the ground.

When doubts overtake you, think of Me.
Those whose hope is in My name
Will not be put to shame.
When doubts overtake you, think of Me.

Psalm 25:3 No one whose hope is in you will ever be put to shame.

When you're coming home to heaven, think of Me.
I'll bring you safely there;
My Son I didn't spare,
So you'd come home to heaven safe with Me.

John 3:16 For God so loved the world that he gave his one and only Son, that whoever believes in him shall not perish but have eternal life.

Old Glory Flies High Today

Let us be the first to say,
"Welcome home to American soil!"
You've kept Old Glory flying,
That mission – never a small toil.

We've dreamed of it – we'll relive it, too –
Right now, standing here,
Seeing our brave loved ones home –
A moment in time held dear.

We saw you off and placed you in
God's almighty hands,
Praying if it was His will,
He'd bring you home again.

Continued…

With humble hearts we bow our heads,
And thank our God above,
For going along on the mission,
For returning those we love.

For the lost, the wounded,
The debt we could never repay,
But we speak for many,
As these words we say:

We the people thank you
For your sacrifices made.
Our land remains free – because you are brave –
Old Glory flies high today.

Saluting America's Finest

Let us do the honors,
Of saluting you today,
Each one – America's finest –
Sacrificial love on display.

Through your dedication and valor,
You've brought honor to life,
Shown courage in the face of terror,
Strength in the face of strife.

Fly high on wings of freedom,
You've defended for each of us.
Fly high knowing you've made a difference,
Many Americans deeply touched.

And then fly home to those you love;
Enjoy peaceful sleep tonight,
Worn out from the lengths to which we've gone,
To make you feel honored on this flight.

Time Will Never Fade

With loving care it's folded,
With somber hearts it's laid,
Into your hands with gratitude
That time will never fade.

You grieve not alone,
Your country with you stands.
Old Glory's wrapped in the love
Of a free and mourning land.

A prayer with the flag is given
Of thanks to our Gracious God,
For the faithful service of this soldier
Who, with every step he trod...

Walked upright with honor,
Protecting the Stars and Stripes,
And for you, who supported his mission
To put country above his life.

With loving care it's folded,
With somber hearts it's laid,
Into your hands with gratitude
That time will never fade.

An American's Prayer

Dear Father, protect the soldier,
Whom I love so dear.
Watch over him night and day;
Guard his heart from fear.

Hold him in Your mighty hand,
And those with whom he serves.
Bind them close together,
Trusting in Your Word.

To leaders give Your wisdom,
As we pray they look to You,
In the details of their missions,
Unified in all they do.

Bring Your peace into this world,
Into the hearts of men.
Convict those bent on evil;
Melt hearts with Your love for them.

Continued…

By the power of Your Spirit,
Touch their lives with grace.
Change them from the inside out,
With love replace the hate.

Heal the wounds inflicted,
On bodies, hearts, and minds.
Draw the hurting close, Lord,
Their hope in You to find.

Please watch over the families
Of those deployed today.
Fill their loneliness, meet their needs,
Keep them strong, we pray.

Help all our soldiers and veterans
To know they're not alone,
We thank You, God, for each of them,
And that freedom reigns at home.

In Jesus' name we pray,
Amen.

About the Author

Julie (Schmidt) Dueker is a Christian educator who loves sharing her passion for God, music, and patriotism with children of all ages. In 2017, Julie was honored as Iowa's VFW Elementary Teacher of the Year. Julie is the founder and director of Young Patriots Club, a Christian ministry of freedom–loving youth whose mission is to honor God and uplift American heroes. She and her young patriots perform at various events honoring heroes by reciting historical documents, singing patriotic songs, and sharing poetry, including the poems in this book.

Julie and her husband, Craig, live in West Des Moines, Iowa, where they have been blessed with the honor of raising three amazing young men, Ryan, Josh, and Zach. Julie is grateful for the support of her family, friends, school family, and Young Patriots Club who share gratitude for God's blessings upon our country, and those whose sacrifices secure our freedoms. For more information about this book, accompanying music, and to learn about Julie's ministries, visit www.juliedueker.com.

About the Illustrator

Ray "Bubba" Sorensen II is nationally and internationally known for his painting of The Freedom Rock®. The Freedom Rock® is a boulder in rural Adair county in Iowa, painted as a heartfelt tribute thanking our nation's veterans, and honoring their service to our country. Bubba has painted The Freedom Rock® with different tributes to our nation's veterans for Memorial Day each year since 1999. Bubba is painting a smaller Freedom Rock® in all 99 Iowa counties, telling a story unique to that geographical location. Bubba is working on the 50–State Freedom Rock Tour, painting a unique–to–their–state Freedom Rock for all 50 states in America.

Bubba has tremendous support of family and friends, most importantly from his wife Maria (Galanakis) and their daughter, Independence, and son, Michael. Bubba and Maria's mural painting business, Sorensen Studios, is located in Greenfield, Iowa. Maria and Bubba work collaboratively to thank veterans one painting at a time. For more information about Bubba and his artwork, visit www.thefreedomrock.com.

WestBow Press books may be ordered through booksellers or by contacting:

WestBow Press
A Division of Thomas Nelson & Zondervan
1663 Liberty Drive
Bloomington, IN 47403
www.westbowpress.com
1 (866) 928–1240

Because of the dynamic nature of the Internet, any web addresses or links contained in this book may have changed since publication and may no longer be valid. The views expressed in this work are solely those of the author and do not necessarily reflect the views of the publisher, and the publisher hereby disclaims any responsibility for them.

Interior Illustration Credit: © 2018 Ray "Bubba" Sorensen II

Author Photo: Ryan Dueker Photography
Illustrator Photo: Maria Sorensen

Scripture quotations marked NIV are taken from The Holy Bible, New International Version®, NIV® Copyright © 1973, 1978, 1984, 2011 by Biblica, Inc.® Used by permission. All rights reserved worldwide.

ISBN: 978–1–9736–6456–7 (sc)
ISBN: 978–1–9736–6457–4 (e)

Library of Congress Control Number: 2019906161

Print information available on the last page.

WestBow Press rev. date: 6/27/2019

WestBow
PRESS®
A DIVISION OF THOMAS NELSON
& ZONDERVAN

Printed in the United States
By Bookmasters